Stop Working, Start Living

Powerful Tips for Entrepreneurs and Employees on How to Get Rich Using the Internet

By: Mark Walker

9781635012828

I0510856

PUBLISHERS NOTES

Disclaimer – Speedy Publishing LLC

This book was originally printed before 2014. This is an adapted reprint by Speedy Publishing LLC with newly updated content designed to help readers with much more accurate and timely information and data.

Speedy Publishing LLC

40 E Main Street, Newark, Delaware, 19711

Contact Us: 1-888-248-4521

Website: http://www.speedypublishing.co

REPRINTED Paperback Edition: 9781635012828:

Manufactured in the United States of America

DEDICATION

This book is dedicated to my joy and pain, my wife, Maria...

TABLE OF CONTENTS

CHAPTER 1- THE NO-SHORTCUT RAGS TO RICHES FAIRYTALE

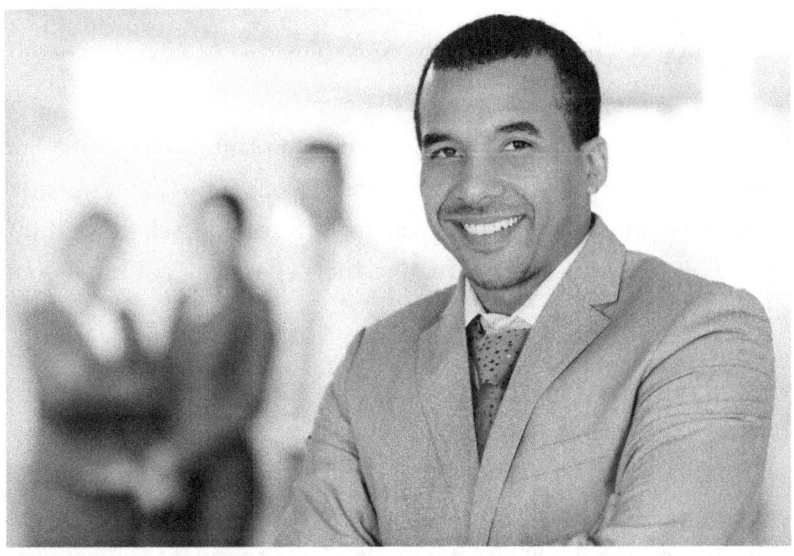

From rags to riches – it happens more often than you might think. In fact, it could be you! Are you content with life as it is or do you find yourself dreaming your way to riches? If you answered yes, then you are definitely on the right track because without your imagination – without dreaming – you are not going to get there!

Have you ever wondered why some people with equal opportunities land up in very different places – with one person living in wealth with all the comforts of home, while the other person struggles to even pay his rent. Why the difference? It's really quite simple, yet for far too many it remains a mystery – it's all about what you are thinking.

If that sounds confusing, you aren't alone! The trouble is we actually create our reality but what we are thinking and dreaming. Here's a question. When you are talking with friends or family, how do you describe yourself? Your life? Are you always talking about how you struggle? Are you saying things like "I was never meant to be rich?" or are you talking about how successful you are how great life is how you have so much abundance. Which describes you? If you are the latter, you are in great shape. However, if you are the person who sees yourself as struggling, that's exactly where you will stay.

We all have ideas from our childhoods implanted deep into our subconscious and if you want to change your future, you need to reprogram your subconscious. You need to see yourself as wealthy, having all that you desire, creating the riches that will fulfill your dreams.

Every thought that makes its way to your subconscious through any one of your senses is recorded and filed in your brain. You can voluntarily implant any thought you would like into your mind and your subconscious will act on it. Your subconscious will dominate your desires and it will direct you. You have complete control over your subconscious mind and so you set yourself up for failure or success – for living the life of a poor person or the life of a rich person.

You simply need the stimuli to influence your subconscious mind to go in the direction you desire. You simply need to imprint your desires in your mind and then have the faith that your desires will become your reality. So start dreaming big today and tomorrow you can enjoy the riches.

Realizing Your Dream in 6 Easy Steps

1. Fix in your mind what you desire. It needs to be an exact picture. It's not enough to say, for example, "My desire is for tons of money." Even be definite about the amount.

2. Decide precisely what you plan to give in return for what you desire. There is no such thing as something for nothing.

3. Determine an exact date that you intend to possess the desired thing by.

4. Design a precise plan to carry out your desire and then begin to get to work immediately, whether you feel ready or not to put your plan into action.

5. Write out a clear and concise statement responding to the four steps above.

6. Two times a day, read your written statement aloud. Once, just after you get up in the morning and once just before you go to bed at night. As you are reading, visualize, feel and believe you already possess whatever your goal is.

Why Believing is the First Step to Getting Rich

Do you want to grow rich? But do you really want to grow rich? How motivated are you? Over the years, there have been many books and speakers telling you how to grow rich, so why then isn't everyone that has read one of these books or listened to one of these speakers wealthy? That's because in order to become rich you need the power of your mind behind you! Let's look at some of the actions you need to take in order to grow rich and enjoy wealth.

#1 Understand the Power of Your Subconscious Mind

It is important that you understand the importance of the power of your subconscious mind. When you set your goals first thing in the morning and at night before bed, you can actually reprogram your brain and you will teach yourself to focus on what it is you want – to grow rich. It will become imprinted on your mind and therefore constantly be focused on methods to get rich. You will find that your belief system is reprogrammed and that includes how you use your money and energy to help you grow wealthy.

#2 Identify the Negative Beliefs You Have About Money

What do you believe about money? Do you have a preconception about money and wealth that might stop you from achieving your goal to grow rich? There are many negative beliefs associated with money. Some of them include:

• Money doesn't grow on trees
• Rich people tend to be mean, dishonest, superficial and bad
• I'm no business person
• If he/she has that kind of money they must be doing something illegal
• Spirituality and wealth do not go together
• I'm just too young (too old) to make a bunch of money
• Others know the secrets around creating wealth but I don't

You need to learn how to spot these negative thoughts when they jump into your head. You should make a list of the thoughts you know you've had. They could be different from the list of examples. You shouldn't feel bad because you have these thoughts, but what you do need to do is change your subconscious belief system. Hire a life coach; talk with people that have enjoyed success and built wealth and change how you think about money, wealth and how it relates to you and how you think.

Chapter 2 - How Millionaires Earned Their Millions

People like Warren Buffet, Bill Gates, and Mark Zuckerberg didn't go to university for years, they didn't earn a degree, and yet they are some of the wealthiest people on the planet. So what do they know that you don't?

They know that you need to dream big. You need to imagine what it is you want and how you want to get there. You need to put that to paper and train your subconscious to think the way the new you thinks. These men had a desire and they were motivated to act on it. They were not scared they would fail and they never gave up. They remained persistent from the beginning.

None of them came from wealthy backgrounds. None of them had lived a life of wealth previously, which means they also had lots of negative baggage going on in their subconscious but they were ready to teach their subconscious a new way of thinking and they were ready to live the dream. They did not see themselves as poor or struggling. They did not see themselves as 'stuck.' Not at all — they picked up their idea and they ran with it — the end result wasn't just success, it was amazing success making them some of the richest people in the world.

Great news! You can be a Bill Gates or Mark Zuckerberg too. Now I know what you're thinking. I don't have any great ideas like they did. What you need to recognize is that it doesn't matter what your idea is to achieve wealth as long as it is unique (i.e. don't open a coffee shop that's just like Starbucks) and there is a demand for what you are offering. You also need to remember there are different ways to achieve wealth and so you need to think about what's right for you.

You need to really want it — You can't just dream about what it might be like to be rich. You have to have the desire in your heart and in your mind. You have to want it so bad you are motivated to do whatever it takes to get there and you aren't going to quit when you run into stumbling blocks (and you will) along the way. You are going to need to be ready to take some risks when the potential outweighs the loss, and you are going to need to be ready to get in there and make it happen.

You need to understand what success really means. Success isn't just about having so much money you never have to worry again. Success isn't about getting a hospital wing named after you because you gave them money to help build it, because there's no real love there. Success is about what you can with that money to help better the world and others around you. Look at the Bill and Melinda Gates Foundation or what U2, Opera or Angelina Jolie has done. These are people that have enjoyed success because their monuments are not about them but rather about others.

Warren Buffet is estimated to be worth over $60 billion dollars and he is the richest man in the entire world (sorry Bill Gates), but how did he get there. Was it luck? Absolutely not! Buffett credits his success to a number of key strategies so let's have a look at some of them.

1. You need to reinvest your profits – In the beginning when you are first starting to make money you may be tempted to spend it. You'll need to resist and instead turn around and reinvest your profits. Warren Buffet figured this out very early because by the time he was 26 he was worth $174,000 and in today's market that's equal it $1.4 million

2. You need to be willing to be different – You cannot base the decisions you are making on what others are doing or saying. When Buffett began to manage his money, back in 1956 he refused to tell anyone where he was putting his money and everyone (including his parent) was sure that he would fail. They were wrong. Buffett looks at what others are doing and sees that as the average and he's not willing to be average. However, in order to not be average you must think and act differently than those who are average.

3. Make sure you spell out the deal clearly before you begin. You have the most bargaining power before you start any job or project. That's when you have what the other party wants. That's the time to sit down and work out all the fine details. Make sure it's in writing. You'd be surprised how many people will go back on their word once they have what they want.

4. Watch the little expenses – The big expenses are obvious but it's the small purchases that will eat up your budget and put you in the poor house. Use what you have wisely and reduce the waste as much as possible, because waste leads to lost wealth.

5. Be careful how much you borrow – It's best to not borrow at all. If you are living on your credit cards and your personal loans, you are never going to get rich. In fact, you are never going to get out of debt. If you find yourself in this mess it's time to negotiate with creditors to pay whatever you can. Then once you are out of debt, begin to start to save.

Five simple things you can do to help you find wealth! Why not start today?

Use Your Imagination to Grow Rich

What's your imagination doing today? Are you thinking about doing that load of laundry when you get home or fixing that broken chair? Or are you dreaming of going on a cruise in the high seas in your beautiful yacht while your crew caters to your every need? Your imagination can make you rich or it can leave you stuck in the rut you live in today. You should never be afraid to dream big and envision your future with wealth and riches.

You are the only one in control of your destiny and that's something many of us forget as we get caught up in our day-to-day lives that are filled with work, family, struggles, and financial woe. No one is going to hand you wealth and if you are hoping to win the lottery, you're likely going to be disappointed. You certainly aren't going to grow rich working for another person, but you'll likely help to make them grow rich. Where do you want to put your energy? Are you going to focus on doing a great job at working and helping your company owner to grow rich or are you going to focus on doing a great job for your own business and making yourself rich? The choice is yours.

Now it takes a lot more than walking out the door of your current employer to find wealth. You need to have a dream and a desire.

What's your dream? What do you want to be doing 10 years from now? Great you have the dream now do you have the desire? Do you have the drive to figure out a way to get yourself there? Use your imagination and don't be afraid to think outside the box. There are plenty of opportunities awaiting you.

Growing rich is also not one of those 'get rich overnight' schemes. If you are looking for an easy way that requires no work, you are not going to make it to wealth. Growing rich doesn't mean you work your fingers to the bone but it does require you to participate and be a part of the process. It does require you to turn your vision, your dream, into a reality and to direct others so that it can happen.

Bottom line – never be afraid to imagine. Use that power to grow rich and create the wealth you desire. You are in control of your future and your destiny. What will your future look like?

Forget the Money, Focus on the Wealth

Making money and enjoying wealth are two very different things, yet far too many of us associate the two as being the same thing. If your goal is to create wealth for yourself, it will help you to understand what wealth looks like. Wealth is ancient whereas money is actually a rather new invention.

Wealth is the things you want – clothes, food, houses, travel to different places, cars, gadgets, and on it goes. Many people don't realize that you can have wealth and not have money. If you had a piece of technology that could create your every whim on demand, you could create a car, a yacht or whatever your desire was without ever having money. If you lived in the farthest corner of the planet in isolation where there was nothing to purchase it wouldn't make any difference the amount of money you have

Wealth is about what you want, not about money. So why do we all focus on money then? That's because in our modern world money is a way to get to wealth – they become interchangeable. It gets even more complicated because when we discuss 'making money' it becomes more difficult for most of us to understand how to make money.

Money is actually a side effect of a world that has become very specialized. For example, in our specialized world, you might need paper but you don't have the tools to make it. You might need a place to live but you have to acquire that from someone else. If you want you must buy your food from someone else. Therefore, you need a way to be able to obtain those goods and services from the other person.

In the past, the barter system was used. But then life was much simpler. You might have grown potatoes and your neighbor might have had wood. You would trade potatoes for wood. You would then trade potatoes for carpenter skills and that's how wealth was built back by our ancestors. However, problems arose when you had potatoes (or whatever your commodity was) and the other person didn't want what you wanted or need. That left you having to trade your commodity for something the other person wanted and then you could trade with them. We've simplified things in the modern world. We now use money, which is the medium of exchange. This allows trade to work effectively and for people to acquire wealth faster, because you essentially have streamlined the process. So you see money is only a tool to get wealth, which can be built many ways.

It's How You Think!

Gina Rinehart is the richest women in the world and she will be the first to point out that the jealousy of the middle class is unjustified. They are middle class because they are more interested in drinking, socializing and taking care of their personal desires rather than working towards their wealth. What is her point? It is really quite simple. Average middle class people think differently than rich people do.

It is not actually about money but rather about attitude. The middle class are busy telling others to be happy and content with what they have, whereas the rich are never content with what they have. Let's look at 4 ways rich people think differently.

#1 Rich people think poverty is the root of all evil whereas other people think money is at the root of all evil. Most people are brainwashed into thinking rich people are either dishonest or lucky.

#2 Rich people believe selfishness is a virtue whereas other people believe it is a vice. Middle class people see the idea that the rich are out there enjoying life as negative. It is this kind of mentality that will keep you from becoming wealthy.

#3 Rich people have a mentality based on action whereas other people have a mentality based on winning the lottery. The majority of people are just waiting for the day that they choose the right numbers and prosperity finds them, but the rich don't think like that. Instead, they are busy looking for ways to create wealth themselves. They aren't waiting around.

#4 Rich people believe wealth is linked to acquiring the right knowledge whereas other people think that the road to wealth is through formal education. Many of the wealthiest people that have done the best have hardly any formal education. The masses of people are convinced that they need their master's and doctorate degrees in order to obtain wealth, because they are locked into thinking linear. The wealthy people aren't looking for a means. They are looking only for the end results. They aren't concerned about a formal piece of paper, only the specific knowledge they need to create wealth.

That's just four different ways that the rich think differently than other people. It's what sets average earners apart from wealthy earners. The way you think is important in the direction your finances go.

CHAPTER 3- CLEAN AND HONEST WAYS TO GET RICH – FAST!

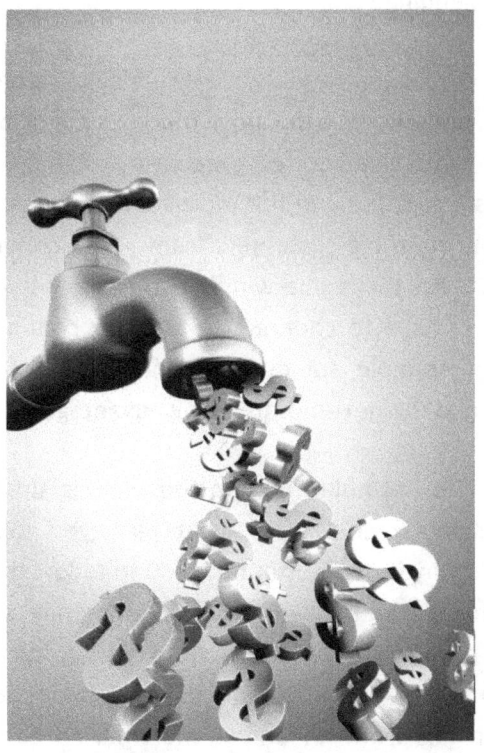

The secret to achieving real wealth is in your hands. If it's really what your heart desires you will make it happen, but if it's something your head talks about but your heart doesn't connect to it will likely never become your reality.

Reaching wealth requires you to have amazing success and that requires not only hard work but smart work. It also requires you to have the stomach to be able to take risks, the persistence to push through and overcome obstacles that get in your way and the strength to take rejection. You are going to have to know your industry.

One thing that every person has achieved wealth has in common is that they have learned how to cut their losses fast and to run with the winners. They've also learned when to recognize the run with the winners is ending.

You need to be able to find the winning strategies for your investment whether that's the stock market or your business. Let's say that you run a small coffee shop and you've learned that the best business is first thing in the morning and you've learned how to up sell your morning customers from just a coffee to a coffee and a bagel. Great that's one winning strategy but you can't let it end there. You have to continue to look for continuous winning strategies. For example, spend one month building your presence on Facebook and the next month taking advantage of coupons.

This is a simple example. The bottom line is the markets are changing constantly no matter what path you take to finding wealth. That's why it is important for you to follow through on any winning strategies and give it the time, money and attention necessary to maximize its value. You also need to stick the strategy long term and keep using it as long as it is working for you. Some winning strategies work for only a short period but others work year after year. It depends on how you are making your wealth.

What is known for sure is that riches follow the person who trusts what they know and figures out how to maximize their effectiveness, while at the same time diligently expanding those winning strategies to continue to grow your income streams and therefore your wealth.

The secret is simple – if wealth is where your heart is then you will focus on creating that wealth.

Valuable Tips to Growing Rich

Are you tired of showing up to a job where you are under appreciated? Are you finished with giving it all you have at work so that someone else gets rich? Are you done with living paycheck to paycheck? If you answered yes to anyone of these questions, you may have a desire for a different kind of life – you may have the desire to grow rich.

Bottom line – If you really want to grow rich you must have desire. Just thinking about it and dreaming about it won't get you there. Of course, you should always dream big and picture what your life will look like once you achieve wealth, but make sure you have the desire or the drive to reach your goals.

"The starting point of all achievement is desire."

We often make the mistake of thinking that in order to grow rich we need to head off to university and get a degree in 'something.' Actually, nothing could be further from the truth. Some of the wealthiest people in the world have no formal education. Hill says, "Education comes from within; you get it by struggle and effort and thought." Life is your education. On your road to riches, you might stumble and fall not once but many times and you need to stand up, dust yourself off, and try again taking away the lesson from your past failure. The education you need to grow rich is learning how others have become rich in the past. Discovering how they have achieved wealth.

"The majority of men meet with failure because of their lack of persistence in creating new plans to take the place of those which fail."

Stop Working, Start Living

If you don't have the persistence to pick up the pieces and try again, you aren't going to make it to becoming rich. Because the truth is, everyone fails (well almost everyone) and you will too and you must be able to make new plans, come up with a new game plan – that's the secret to growing rich.

"Failure is a trickster with a keen sense of irony and cunning. It takes great delight in tripping one when success is almost within reach"

Think about it – you had a failure, but what if success was just a step further and you caved in and gave up on your dream to be rich. Sadly, this happens every day. If you want to be rich, you can – no one can stop you. It's within you. Do you have the desire to make it happen?

Everyone has a desire to be rich, but actually only a few get there. Why is that? Many would like to believe it's because others are luckier than they are, and while that might be the case for the minority that win the lottery or inherit a fortune, that's not the case for most. Getting rich requires desire, dedication, skill, and patience. You must be ready to take a risk and weather the storm those followers. Getting rich doesn't happen overnight, but you can make it happen. You can have that life you dream of.

1. Dream big – It begins with having a dream. Write it down; create a mind map of what your life will look like when you are wealthy. Know what it is you want and how you think you'll get there. It's not good enough just to have wishful thinking. Your dream needs to resemble reality and that starts with your imagination.

2. Live within your means – One of the biggest mistakes people make is to live beyond what their true means are and credit has made that possible. The trouble is there is no hope of you ever

getting out of your vicious cycle if all your earnings go to service your debt. You might be surprised to learn that wealthy people live within their means. Now from our point of view that looks pretty luxurious but because of their wealth, it's well within their means. They however, are not busy running up credit card debt.

3. Own your own business – As long as you keep working for someone else you will not become rich. You will simply help to make the owner of the company you work for rich. Instead take that energy and put it into creating your own wealth and creating your own destiny.

4. Be ready to take a risk – No risk no gain no wealth. It's really that simple. There's no sure way to get rich. However, there is a sure way not to get rich and that's to be too scared to take a risk that something will succeed.

5. Don't be scared – Fear will kill all dreams and it will kill all desire. If you are scared you won't be willing to take the risks. As well, if you are living in fear you are feeding your subconscious negative emotions and you will never get out from under your current situation until you retrain your subconscious and that requires positive emotions.

You have the ability to get rich – each and every one of us does. The question is whether we act on the dream.

Think like a Millionaire

You've heard it before – you are what you eat, well that methodology also applies to your financial well-being. Think small you'll live small and struggle with a small income. Think big, you'll live big and find yourself with an abundance of wealth.

Stop Working, Start Living

Now don't confuse living big with living extravagantly and beyond your means. Live big means you focus on your wealth and on being wealthy, you don't spend your days counting your pennies and worrying about where your next dollar will come from. You know that you will have an abundance of money – you spend time dreaming about how you will use your wealth – where you will live, where you will travel – you think big. That constant focus will guide you in the right direction and help you to achieve your goals.

Of course, it's going to take a lot more than just sitting their dream. You'll be disappointed if all you do is meditate your day away envisioning your big pile of green backs. But desire will motivate you to reach your wealth. If you are content with the humdrum 9 to 5 waiting for the next paycheck knowing full well that you'll be broke before you even get that check, then that's the life you are destined to. But if you are not content with that, if your desire is to have the freedom to do what you want, to see what the world has to offer, to live like a millionaire, to travel the world, then you'll have the desire to make that happen. Your imagination is important.

Again, if your imagination and desire of being wealthy is limited to dreaming about what numbers you'll pick on next week's lottery ticket, you're still missing what it takes to grow rich.

Imagination and self-motivation go hand in hand. Look at some of the wealthiest people and their stories and you'll find that long before they were wealthy they were already dreaming about what they could have done better, what they could have done more efficiently – they were motivated.

Finally, you'll need to make some decisions. If you are going to grow rich, you simply can't sit on the fence trying to decide – you'll need to make decisions right or wrong. The wrong decisions aren't a waste because they should be seen as lessons. When you make up your mind, make sure you stick to it. Opinions are everywhere. In fact, on the entire planet, they are the cheapest commodity to be found. So, don't let other peoples' opinions affect you.

How many how to e-book have you read on getting rich? Would an aspiring millionaire actually spend their money to buy these book or would they hang on to their seed money worried that they would run short before they even got started. Great news – if you are reading and investing in books on how to be successful and how to grow wealth you are on the right track. After all, some of the best books on the market have studied millionaires and their methodology is based on just that, because really if you want to be a millionaire who better to study?

Most millionaires have been right in some of the things they've done and some of been right in most of what they've done. Past that, you might be surprised to discover there isn't that much different between their stories of success.

You might be surprised to learn that you could very well have a millionaire as a neighbor. Most millionaires do not lead extravagant lives. They live comfortable but they watch for sales, use coupons, buy in bulk, search for deals, refinish rather than replacing their furniture, and they are very practical, even frugal, in nature. As their wealth grows, they remain that way.

Another common trait among millionaires is that they are not afraid to take risk. Don't mistake this for taking foolish risks on get rich schemes. On the contrary – they do their research and take calculated risks on what they believe will make them money. But they do lose to and they are willing to take that risk. If they fail, they don't quit. They dust themselves off and they go at it again.

Millionaires know how to dream big. They knew how to dream big long before they were a millionaire and this keeps them focused on making more money not spending less. You can save half of what the guy next door saves and still end up ahead thanks to what's often referred to as 'silly behavior' in investing. Translated this means you are busy chasing the next get rich investment rather than investing in an index fund and investing small amounts every month to average your costs of investment.

It seems the essential ingredients in the recipe to wealth are to begin with inspiration and focus. Once you start to enjoy the money coming in you spend less than you make (that means no living on credit cards) and then you take those savings and you invest them wisely. It's really that simple.

CHAPTER 4- THE RELATIONSHIP BETWEEN YOUR EMOTIONS AND YOUR FINANCIAL FUTURE

So you want to be rich, but how well are you doing at achieving your goal? You may be surprised to learn that your own emotions are what are either holding you back or creating the riches you desire. Let's explain further.

According to hundreds of others who have created success and become rich, you must make your sure that your desires are clearly stated. You should also make sure to write down your desires. In addition to determining your desires, you need to have the persistence to carry out the instructions to achieve your desires.

Remember, your subconscious mind is always functioning even when you make no effort to influence it. If you want to benefit your subconscious mind, you need to make sure you are feeding it positive emotions and not negative ones. If you think about fear and poverty most of the time, then that's the life your mind is conditioning you to live. You are the master of your impulses and you must learn to feed them the desired food to ensure you get the desired results.

Your subconscious is never idle. If you don't take the time to send your desires to your subconscious, it will feed on the negative thoughts that go through your mind. Both negative and positive impulses will reach your mind and create your destiny.

By using your controlled imagination you can create plans and focus on purpose that will lead you to success. Everything that we do starts with an impulse. Humankind creates nothing that does not begin with a thought. When you add in the imagination, you can train your subconscious to create the success you desire.

Be careful because the mind is easily influenced by impulses or any thought that is mixed with emotion or feeling. In fact, there is a great deal of research that would indicate the only thoughts that become actions are those that have emotion associated with them.

You are writing the script and the audience is your subconscious. The response of your audience will depend on the emotional message you deliver and how you influence your subconscious audience. You need to speak the language it can understand. There are seven positive emotions that are keys to your subconscious. They are:

• Desire
• Faith

- Hope
- Love
- Sex
- Romance
- Enthusiasm

There are others but these are the most powerful if you want to see your desires become reality.

There are also seven negative emotions that you need to avoid. They are:

- Jealousy
- Fear
- Hatred
- Greed
- Revenge
- Superstition
- Anger

If you get caught up in these emotions, you will never reach your desires. You will never become rich. So how will you handle your emotions? Are you going to make it to rich?

CHAPTER 5- HOW TO DEVELOP THE RIGHT MILLIONAIRE MINDSET

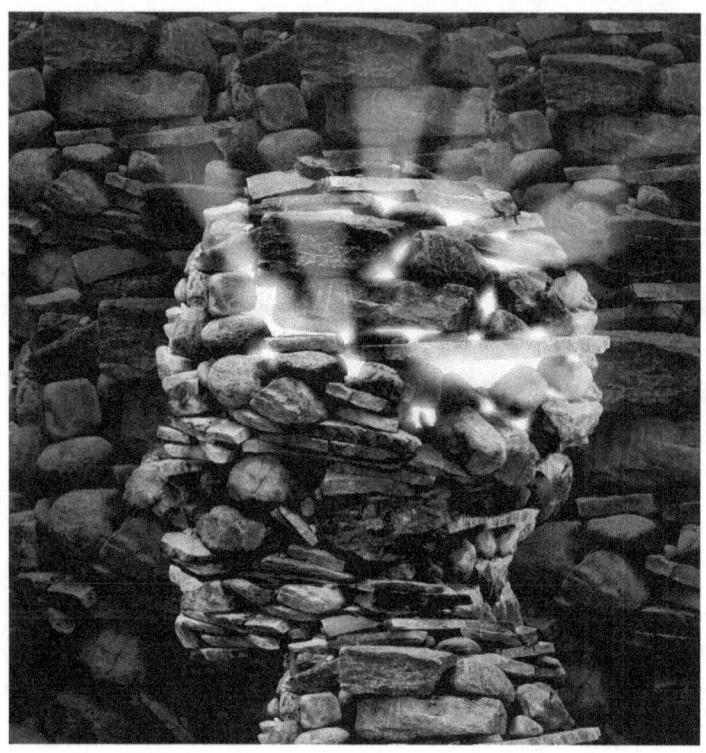

Everything major plan or big business has a birth place – that is from the mind (the source where every action flows out from).

Before you jump into the Internet marketing scene, one of the first things that you must fine-tune is your mindset.

But what does it mean to develop the right mindset? Here are a few suggestions:

Making money online is NOT a get rich quick scheme. You don't just 'dump money' into some marketing scheme hoping to get money in return.

You must invest time into your education. Depending on your aptitude, you don't just read an E-book or two and expect to become an Internet marketing expert. After all, how long did it take you to get your university degree?

You must invest time for trial and error. No one gets it 'right' on the first try. You must be prepared for failures and mistakes. Learn from them and make sure you get up and fight again!

You must be prepared to put up with negative people. There are many in the world out there who do not believe that it is possible to make money online. When you put your plans into action, you will face resistance from your beer-drinking buddies, your family members and/or even your BOSS! If you don't have the endurance, you will succumb to the pressure.

You must be prepared to go all the way. An Internet marketing business is just like any other business in the 'offline' world. If you are not prepared to go all the way, you will give up halfway because you have put in a half-hearted attitude into your business. Remember the golden rule: how badly do you want success?

Another thing that you must remember is that it is not enough to have the winning mindset alone. You must have the right vehicle to take you there. For example: if you are wanted to get from one state in the U.S. to another, you will need to have the right vehicle to take you there. You can choose to ride a plane, drive a car or walk.

Of course it would be absurd to walk. But that is what people do in their Internet marketing business! They do not choose the best (or cost effective) vehicle to get them there!

They have the right mindset alright. And they are probably so fired up and positive that they don't care how long it takes them to arrive at their destination.

It is also no different from natives who are all riled up about defending their homeland against invaders, but if they don't have guns, their axes, spears and shields are not going to save them no matter how valiantly they fight (against the enemy's gunpowder)!

Make no mistake about this. Taking too long to reach the destination is no different from failing. We must not delude ourselves into thinking that it takes time to build a business when we should be making money after a couple of months.

Some people spent years reading 'make money online' E-books without making a single cent from the Internet. They convince themselves that they are still in the learning and education phase but they don't take action!

Sure it takes time to build a solid business, but any money that you are not making means you've 'lost' money because that is the money that you SHOULD be earning instead of wasting your time with things that don't work.

Your Own Personalized Roadmap to Success

Find a proven business model

There are currently many business models running on the Internet. As a newbie, your goal is to start making money as fast as possible while taking as little time as possible to achieve it.

This is your vehicle to success!

Look for a business model that people have already made money from.

Here are a few suggestions:

Resell Rights – how you can sell other people's products and keep 100% of the profit while getting viral marketing traffic at the same time.

Private Label Rights – brand yourself by having 100% ready to go products in your own name!

Product Launches – how to conduct a five figure launch properly.

Niche Marketing – find good niche markets to make money online

Google AdWords – a complete Google AdWords blue print to help you maximize your Pay-per-click campaigns

Making Sales With Graphics – how to use graphics to enhance your sales letters.

These are just a few examples that you can check out.

Remember that no matter what business model you choose, always remember to think long term, work hard (and smart) and bring value to your customers.

Stop Acting like an Inventor, Just Follow the Trends

One common mistake newbies make when it comes to Internet marketing is to try things that might not work.

They come up with their own ways to make money online but what they don't realize is that many marketers have already perfected the formula of making money online that all they need to do is emulate what they are doing.

Most newbies fail because they spend too much trial and error and they get discouraged because they do not see the results.

The best way is to pick a marketer that is already making money and just follow their systems (or invest in their packages) – at the very least, you can get a refund within 30 days if it doesn't work (but don't use the refund policy as a way out just because you are LAZY).

How to Obtain Your Needed Information

In the Stone Age, information was obtained through observation. We saw that it turned bright and dark alternately. We observed that was a regular phenomenon that happened without a break. The concept of day was born. We realized that when two pieces of flint are rubbed together, they can create a spark. We learned how to make fire. We understood that water pours from the sky in the form of rain, and we can shelter ourselves in caves. The first homes were created. We understood that man and woman can mate and create progeny. We understood that people united in this manner should stay together for their various needs. The concept of family was born. We understood that families can do better if they huddle together. They can fight natural calamities and predating animals in a better manner. Communities were born.

Later we understood that we could plant seeds in the ground and crops came up. We learned our first method of sustenance. Then we had free time. We realized that we had an artistic instinct. We could create things of beauty. The first rock paintings were just a precursor to our different art forms. Our monosyllabic sounds evolved into language.

Throughout this evolutionary process, we acquired information all the way. There was no one to teach us; it was only our keen sense of observation that got us going. But, we did not stop at that. That is what makes us different from animals around us. We have a talent, a special skill, for taking what we have and trying to improve it all the time. So, we took our innate genius of observation ahead. We began to observe both in the micro world and in the macro world. We saw things smaller than our eyes could see and we saw things more distant than our vision could see. We understood that microorganisms exist; we understood that there is space. We tried to hear things that our ears did not allow us to listen. We understood there are infrasonic waves and we understood there are ultrasonic waves.

Today, we are living in times when we know a lot about the world, definitely more than what we knew in the Stone Age. There is still a long way to go... what we know already may not even be the equivalent of an electron in the composition of the entire world, but we know something that's more than what we knew to start with.

This is amazing progress. And, the best thing is that we have not put a stop on our progress yet. We are moving on. Skipping to the present, our patterns of receiving information have definitely evolved to great heights. Today, we do not need to observe to survive. We live in much better times. We are beyond learning merely survival tactics. We are now trying to ameliorate our lives.

Speaking on an individual note, if you need some information on something, you know that you have all the resources you need at your fingertips. The Internet is certainly the most revolutionary invention humankind has achieved so far. It has linked everyone in the world, regardless of time, space and expertise, to become a unified whole. This is an amazing pool of talent and information. Today, if we need something, we just have to dip into this pool and everything is right there.

We still need to obtain information for several things. It is still a routine process for us. We are surging ahead, surely. Things are looking good as well, because there are hardly times when we are stuck for not knowing something that we should. The whole world is tuned in to this channel of information known as the Internet. It is up to us to make the most of it

In present times, if someone needs to know something, the first and most normal thing for them to do is to simply get to their favorite browser and find out information. It does not matter what they are looking for. Whether it is...

• Knowing what a particular term means,
• Getting information on some geographical region of the world,
• Understanding how to do something,
• Reading a review on a product or a service,
• Buying something with the right knowledge about it,
• Finding out ways to earn a livelihood by sitting at home,
• Finding out more about a subject of interest,
• Seeking entertainment...

...or whatever else, there is the Internet at our disposal. Millions of people log in everyday to find out what they want. And there is hardly a time when they are not able to find what they are looking for.

It is such an interesting world that we have created in the virtual realm. People are not just seeking information, but they are giving out information as well. Even the littlest things that they do, such as posting a comment on a blog post that rivets their attention, they are giving out some kind of information to someone. Creating blogs and websites has become much easier than it was when the Internet was just teething. Today, people have personal blogs and websites and they are passionate about them just as people were passionate about their fishing hobby in days of yore. People are setting up these mediums on the Internet and informing and instructing people all the time. It is a continuous process, a process that sees a million new things being fed into the online world with each passing day.

The best thing is the optimism of it all. We know that there is already a humongous lot of information on the Internet. This information is never going to dwindle. At the same time, a humongous amount of information is being added each day that we cross. Our entire knowledge bank is slowly getting transferred onto the Internet. And this is not the knowledge of a single person or a single company or even a single country. It is the knowledge amassed from the whole world... the knowledge that we have earned through generations of our survival on the Internet.

We can easily create a schism for the total time we spent on the earth. Earlier, historians used to refer to prehistory (the time when there were no written records) and historical times (the time of which written records are available). Surely, now historians are going to rethink this and create another schism. They are going to introduce an era of pre-Internet and an era of Internet times. Several centuries down the line, people are going to know us as the people who lived at the very start of the Internet age, and they are going to respect us for it.

You have to understand the massive importance of it all. Due to the Internet, there is a way for us to pass on everything that we know to the future generations. There is not a single thing they will miss out on, not a single nuance. They will know exactly when Obama became president of the US and how, they will know precisely about the launch of the iPhone, they will know who won the NFL Championship and in which year, they will know about Egypt coming out of its dictatorial yoke and in the exact manner that it did so, they will know when Rihanna sang Umbrella, they will know about almost every person living on the earth at every time and what they did for a living and even what their personal likes and dislikes were.

It might sound scary, and it is. If an alien invasion were to happen, they would only need to hack into our WWW to find out almost everything they need to know about us. We are all exposed at the same time. We are vulnerable.

Our sons and daughters will know everything about us, and this information will pass on for generations beyond. The Internet is never going to cease, but it will only ameliorate with time. We will surely be able to do better things, but this collective wealth of information that we have amassed, that we are keeping on amassing as we speak, will never be let down into the drain.

For Everything Else, Use the Internet

It is an understatement actually. All we need is definitely out there, but that does not even comprise of a teensy-weensy fraction of the total amount of information that is present.

There is just so much out there, on the Internet especially, that we cannot make use even of a tiny decimal of it all. But, if you think about it on an individual note, what don't we have on the Internet?

We have everything that we need to survive… even how to make a living in the freezing woods if we want to.

We are living in the Internet age, and that certainly means a lot of things to all of us. For some people, it means that they never have to live without friends. The Internet can always help them socialize. For others, it means that they can buy things from the comfort of their homes.

For some others, it means that they can download movies, music and games for free and get themselves entertained wherever they are. For still some others, it is a means of business, a means of making pots of money and keeping it that way. And then there are people for whom the Internet is a channel for making themselves popular all over the world.

There are so many different manifestations of the Internet that it is enough to make our heads spin just thinking about what we can do with it. There are so many different things that we can do, so many different ways in which we can put the Internet to use. And, the best thing is that we are putting the Internet to use at every living instant of our life. But, we should talk about the greatest purpose of the Internet in our lives, or at least the purpose for which we should actually use the Internet.

To acquire information to do what we want is the one thing that we should revere and worship the Internet for. We have to realize that everything that we need is out here on the Internet. This is the one channel that transmits whatever we want to know about whatever we want to do.

Earlier, children were totally dependent on their parents, teachers and counselors when they were going through the phase of puberty. They were intrigued by the changes happening in their bodies. I am sure many of you have experienced that discomfort as well. We did know why these things were happening and we weren't sure whom to ask. Asking our elders wasn't always an option. And a lot of us heard a lot of wrong things from our friends who had presumably "seen it all".

But, today, children have an option. They save themselves the embarrassment and the inconvenience of it all and they can simply find out about things on the Internet. That is just one example. There are so many others like that. In those days, even a simple anomaly around the house, like a leaking faucet, for example, meant that most people had to call their plumber. And, if the plumber was busy, they had to wait till His Lordship could make it.

Today, that is not the case at all. For such minor things, there are hundreds of DIY guides out there. Better than that, there are vides. You can just see those videos and understand that there are so many things you can do, and how simple it is to do all those things. We are getting so much information at every instant. Whenever we need something, we have a veritable goldmine of information that we can tap into and get whatever we want. It is too fascinating for words!

And, if you want to buy a product, you don't just go out and buy it. Most people will want to do their due research on the Internet first. They will log in to check what other people are saying about the product. Whether it is a movie or a restaurant, we first want to know what other people's experiences with those things have been. We are always interested in reviews. This wasn't the case before the Internet, at least not to this extent, but now we have the information available at out fingertips, so why don't we make the most of it? We surely do!

The one thing that you have to take away from this is that there is almost nothing you will want to know that you won't find on the Internet. The Internet is your biggest source of information right now. It has everything you will need. It does not matter if you want to just eke out a living or you want to do something that can change the course of life as we know it. The information is all out there for you to tap into. You need to only accept that fact and take whatever you can.

What You Can and Cannot Know Online

So, the Internet is a resource of information that you should surely not ignore. But, is it the most complete system there is? Can you find everything you want on it?

Before we go ahead with this discussion, I call upon you to read the title of this chapter once again. The title is "All You Need Is Out There". I am not saying "All You Want Is Out There"!

It is true that you can find everything for your necessities on the Internet. The basic things and much more than that are all out there on the Internet. If there is some information that humankind has found out and if it is supposed to be public knowledge, then you will easily find it.

For instance, if you need to find out about the total population of Trinidad & Tobago and you want to know the demographics of the place, you will find that information quite easily.

If you need to find out about all the books Neil Gaiman ever wrote, you can easily do that. You can even read reviews on those books. You can also find out how to make beef chili yourself. You can learn how to clean your air conditioner. You can understand why gas stove to buy for your picnic. Such is the information that you can easily find.

But then there is a limit. And it is because we need to keep the Internet a safe place more than anything else.

You are not going to find classified information on the Internet. There is no way you can find sensitive information that can put someone or something into jeopardy. If something is illegal, you won't be able to find information on the Internet. And, it is illegal to even look for such information, so you should desist right there!

There is more to that. You won't be able to find personal information on people, especially if the person is not a celebrity. Yes, you might be able to find their profiles or their pictures if they are active on the Internet, but you will not find inside details on them, at least not the details that they don't want to be publicly known.

You will also not be able to find something that has a commercial value; at least you will not find it easily for free. For instance, if someone is selling an eBook, you will likely not be able to find it for free. You will have to buy the book. If a new movie has just been released, you will probably not be able to find it for free unless the producers have streamed the movie themselves or someone has already uploaded a torrent of it. In any case, trying to get things that have a commercial and creative value for free is considered to be illegal, so you have to keep that in mind.

Apart from that, everything that you need is out here on the Internet. You can find things that you need for a good living. In the times we are living, you won't be able to find everything on the Internet, but you will easily find everything that you need to find. But, developments and advancements will always keep on happening and the knowledge base on the Internet is only going to keep growing.

Take from the Internet whatever you can. It is a public resource, available to you and to everyone else on the planet. Make the most of it and you will find that you will be able to enhance your life in various ways. In the subsequent chapters, we are going to talk about how we are going to be able to do just that. So, keep tuned in!

How to Find Out What the Experts Know

One of the most fantastic things that have happened in recent times is the spread of knowledge. There is very little that you cannot know if you set your mind to it. In fact, if you set your mind to it, then you can find out things from the experts themselves. And, if you put in a little more effort, you could find out just what the experts know.

The world of knowledge dissemination has undergone a radical change because of the advent of the Internet. Now, you no longer need to depend on a library book to tell you what to do.

As we have been seeing in the earlier chapters, there are multiple ways in which you can find out information on the Internet. You can find out information on almost every niche that you can think of.

Whether you are trying to look for information on something very popular like how to lose your weight, or you are trying to look information on something that is a very narrow niche like how to solve a problem on integration, you have the accessibility to information.

But, it goes farther than that. If you put your mind into it, you could actually find out things from the experts. You could find out what the specialists of any niche are telling about a particular topic. How fantastic that would be! You can find out things right from the subject gurus.

Our predecessors may have predicted various things about our times, but I don't think they ever thought that the whole world will become this vast intricate network in which information could be available to anyone who wanted it, directly from the people who are an authority on the subject.

So, how do you go about finding information from experts? There are actually several ways to do it.

1. Articles written by experts are available easily on the Internet. These articles pertain to almost every niche conceivable. In a previous chapter, I mentioned several article directories where you could find articles by7 different authors. All these authors are authorities in their particular niches. Almost all of them will have some business that is related with what they write about. This is a way of establishing their credentials. People who run businesses about something are usually the best people to know about that particular thing.

And, it is so convenient. All these articles directories that you can freely find on the Internet have their own search bars. Even if there are millions of articles on the website, you could search for specific information by merely putting in a keyword. Type in the keyword you are looking for information on and hit „Enter" or click on the „Search" button. You will find a host of articles relating to the subject.

2. The second way where you can find information on a particular topic is by looking for a blog on that subject. There are many blogs on almost everything and you could find them easily using Google. Just type the keyword that relates to the blog and type the word „blog" after it. Many blogs will show up. Open up all of them and see what they contain. I am certainly not trying to tell you that all these blogs will be excellent, but you are surely going to find something that you will really like.

In many ways, you will find that blogs are better than articles. Blogs are updated information. Once an article is written, the author will usually forget about it. But this does not happen with a blog. Any blogger will continuously have to update their blog if they have to keep their prospects high. Hence you are going to find new information on your favorite blog almost every time you visit it.

Blogs are also great because you can comment on them. If you like something, you can post your comment on the blog and the blog owner can read it. Even if you detest something, you can write about it on a blog. But, the best thing is that if you want some clarification on something, you can ask the blog poster about it. You can ask them a direct question, and it will mostly be answered. For the blogger, answering your question becomes a way of keeping the blog active. If wanted, they can convert the response to your question into a new blog post itself. This helps them put something on the blog, and hence attract more traffic.

3. Right now, a great way to find information right from the experts is to check out videos on websites like YouTube. You will find entire channels of videos added by experts, who usually have a business that they are trying to promote through these videos. However, that should not bother you. Even if these people have some commercial interest in mind, you should realize that these people have a business about the subject you are looking for information

on. So, you can be a little more accepting of their credibility and their expertise. Moreover, you will find that the videos itself are a great thing. When something is so visual, you can certainly understand it better and you immediately want to put it into use.

Even videos give you the opportunity to ask questions to the creator of the video. You could tell them about something in the comments section that follows the videos. When they read them, they are sure to generate some kind of interest if what you are saying is good information. In fact, you could just read the comments put in by other viewers of Internet. Even that could give you a very good idea of the subject for which you need information.

4. Download eBooks. You are sure to find a veritable goldmine of information in them. EBooks are invariably written by people who know the subject thoroughly. These people have high credibility. Most of the technical eBooks that you will find on the Internet are distributed by online companies and not individuals. The information found in them is rich and useful. You can download eBooks from blogs and websites, which may offer links for the download. It is possible that they will ask you your email id before downloading. There is usually no ulterior motive in this. All they will want to do is to add you to their list so that they can inform you of more products later on. Yes, there is a promotional intention here, but you won't be sold anything to until you agree to purchase it. And, in any case, if you are getting a highly informative eBook out of it, then why should you not go for it?

5. P2P networks are also good places where you can get content from the Internet. There are many such networks where people share content with each other. P2P stands for Peer to Peer. People share all kinds of data with each other here. These could be movies or songs or software application or text material... whatever. Even

the most difficult information can be accessed on P2P networks. You have to download things from these networks and they get saved on your computer. Just make sure that you have a good antivirus program installed because some of these downloads can carry viruses. In any case, if the antivirus program is installed, it will screen the file before it starts downloading. A good P2P network where you can get reliable and safe content is LimeWire. Try it out. There is a huge community here and it keeps on building as we speak. They also have a content filtering system of their own.

6. An extension of the P2P networks is the torrent websites, which are also a place where people share all different types on content. They are networks that are more sophisticated. A lot of people download content from such places, and they may decide to share it with others or not. If they share content with others, then they are called seeders. If they just download content and do not share it with others, they become leechers. All these torrent places have a code of ethics of their own.

If you are taking something from a torrent website, then you will need to have a downloading application such as µtorrent or Bittorrent, which you can easily download from their websites, which are free applications. There are many paid torrent download applications as well, but the free ones will do everything you want. Especially µtorrent is the world's preferred torrent download application. It is known to be the lightest such application, which means it does not put any pressure on your hard disk whatsoever. Before starting, you will need to visit these above websites and download and install these applications onto your computer.

So, if you are looking for any kind of information on a torrent, you just visit Google and type the name of the content followed by torrent. For example, if you are looking for a torrent of the recent movie 127 Hours, you simply have to write 127 Hours torrent" in the search bar in Google and search.

In an instant, you will find several options turning up. Options from reputable torrent websites such as The Pirate Bay and Kickass Torrents will lead the list. Click on these torrent links. Here you can find out a lot of things about the quality of the torrent. You can find out details like the size of the torrent, the number of seeders and leechers that the content has, and maybe even some reviews and comments about the torrent put in by previous downloaders.

This gives you a very good idea whether or not you want to download this content. Also, most of these websites will mention something known as the „health" of the torrent, which tells you how good the torrent is, and you can also find out whether downloading the torrent is a safe proposition for your computer.

In any case, if you hunt for your torrents on the websites I mentioned above, you are almost assured of finding genuine torrents (not fake, spam content) which has already been screened by them to be safe. So, you can go ahead with it easily.

As soon as you click the links of these torrents, they will automatically ask to be saved on your computer in a particular location. You simply have to confirm this (you can change the location if you want) and you will see that the torrent begins downloading in that particular location.

Once that begins happening, you have to just wait till the entire torrent is downloading. This can take some time, depending on the size of the torrent and the number of seeders and leechers that the torrent has.

One problem with torrent downloads is that you can never be sure of the quality of the content (and, in some cases, even if the content is genuine or not) unless and until you have the entire content downloaded on your computer and check it.

That is a major drawback and it can prove to be frustrating to most people. You have to simply wait till the entire content has been downloaded to your computer. You cannot check previews or anything of that sort when it is downloading. You have to merely rely upon the initial description of the content put by the uploader and the reviews and comments that the previous downloaders have given.

But, this is the best way to get content from the Internet that the general public can use. I gave an example of a movie download here, but you can find out just about any content present on earth. People are uploading what they have all the time, and if someone has uploaded some content, then it is possible that you will find it. It is all there; for some things, you may just have to look harder.

7. I always give a lot of importance to the social networking websites for getting great content as well. There have been so many instances when I have found things from these websites. I am present on most of the social networking websites, and even in the websites that I do not use on a regular basis; I have more than 100,000 contacts. I certainly do not know even a tenth of these people, but can you imagine the vast resource pool that I have built up here? All these people are connected to me in some way. Maybe they liked something I wrote or they were part of my business in some way or maybe they are just part of my family and friends. Whatever it is, they are a great resource pool that I have. They are a resource pool that I occasionally tap into to get good informative. And since I have a vast assortment of people here,

there are so many experts on so many subjects that I can approach directly whenever I need them.

If you are looking for a good, professional-type social network to tap into, then you should look for the following two: Twitter and LinkedIn

Not only will you get a huge network of professional people here to connect with, but you will benefit a lot from their expertise. Both of these are professional websites.

The networks are of people who are looking to connect with each other for some or the other business associated reason. They are not together for fun or entertainment or just passing their time as you will find on some of the other networking websites on the Internet, but these people are together for enhancing their business prospects. A lot of these people will talk about their professions directly and will solicit help and guidance for everyone else in their list.

Twitter is also known to be a celebrity haunt. Almost every celebrity worth their salt on this planet is a member of Twitter. They make tweets almost religiously, where they tell people what they want to tell. Sometimes these are self-benefiting (like the tweet made by 50 Cent recently about some stock tips for a company he has interests in) or sometimes they are just for letting people know what they are up to. They also want to find out feedback from people about the various things they are doing.

You could also use Twitter in so many different ways. If you are looking for some information, just tweet about it. You are sure to find a lot of people in your network wanting to help you out. Many people will tell you where you should go to get that information, or they will give you that information yourself.

LinkedIn is slightly different, but very helpful all the same. This is where you make your professional profiles and link with other people. These people become a part of your group; they can recommend you to others and connect with you for any other business associated reason. Your profile on LinkedIn could be a great enhancement to your resume as well.

Nowadays, several employers screen their prospective job applicants on places like LinkedIn so that they get a good idea of what these people are like. It is not just about getting the information you want; it is also about linking with people to enhance your prospects.

For its sheer size of population and its popularity, you may want to consider a profile on Facebook. Chances are that everyone you know is already on Facebook and they are connecting with each other.

You can make a lot of friends here; you can also connect with the friends of your friends and just about anyone. Just get in touch with people and build your network. Whenever you want any information, you have connections with a vast multitude of people. Surely a lot of them are experts in the subject and they will tell you what they know to help you out.

So, these are some of the places where you would like to go to find information, right from the experts. Try them out... you will be surprised at what you can find.

CHAPTER 6- HOW TO USE KNOWLEDGE MARKETING TO GROW YOUR ASSETS

The world of the Internet knows one thing for sure... that knowledge rocks! Information is what sets the world moving! Without the right information, the world's progress as we know it would be seriously impaired. This feeling has given rise to a whole new concept—that of knowledge marketing.

So, why was the Internet invented? That's a good question. We use the Internet so much right now that we hardly give this a thought. The Internet has seeped into almost every area of our lives. Like water or air, we are almost taking its existence for granted. All right, water and air do not undergo technological advancements... they are natural things that will be just like they are since time immemorial... and the Internet is undergoing one new advancement a minute, but then the fact still stands. That the Internet is something that has become so prevalent right now that we use it without giving a second thought about its existence.

The Internet was hardly invented at one particular time in history. It was invented in bits and pieces, so to speak, and then the various small inventions were combined into a large whole that became the World Wide Web. That is how the Internet came into existence. They say that necessity is the mother of invention. That was really proven true in the case of the Internet. It was the need for a stable and secure mode of communication that led to the invention of this medium during the World War 2, which later developed into the Internet. A very preliminary form of the Internet was used during the War to send messages to the troops. This was a highly secure system and it ran in a very closed manner; the outside world had no access to it whatsoever. But, definitely, this was the development of the Internet.

Many different avatars later, and six decades later, we have the Internet as it is in front of us right now. We are using it day in and day out and not giving the slightest thought to the various efforts that went into shaping it the way it has become now.

But, what is important for us to remember at this point is that the Internet is a medium that has grown in utility immensely since those times. In the past, the Internet was just a means of communication. You could consider it to be something like an advancement of a wireless system. That is what it was supposed to be—a highly sophisticated and advanced means of communication that did not fall into the enemy's hands.

And then came the time when people started regarding the Internet in quite another manner altogether. When it went public, it became a source of information. The concept of website was developed. People from all over the world, mostly companies and organizations back then, could make websites and make them live on the Internet. Most corporate entities and other organizations took up this opportunity wholeheartedly. They made their online presence, and started getting in touch with their customers.

The biggest revolution of the Internet came in the nineties. This was the time when the Internet changed from being just a medium of secure communication and converted to being an information highway. This was one of the primary purposes of its existence, but it was not until the dawn of the nineties that it was really put to use.

People now realized that they could share information on the Internet. They realized that the information put into the online world will remain as it is and that they could tap into it whenever they needed. They understood that they could keep this information over the Internet for posterity. Even if civilizations would be wiped out, they could leave their indelible mark on the Internet. Most importantly, people found out that they could use the Internet to find out whatever they wanted to know, regardless of geography, demography, culture or even time. They could visit a country virtually and find out more about it. They could read a book that was never released in their country. They could find out about various nuances of science that they always wanted to find out. They could understand about things that they needed to but did not know whom to ask.

Over the decade, the Internet became a sensation. When the nineties began, people were still quite in the dark about what this invention was and how it could be really harnessed. The organizations were making the most of it, but the common people weren't quite sure what this behemoth was all about. They did not know. There was a factor of intrigue as well, and people did not know what would happen when they used the Internet in particular ways. Taking advantage of the credulousness of people, the Internet crime wave began as well. People suddenly found that money was stolen from their bank accounts and credit cards, that emails were sent to them from all kinds of strange places, that their names were associated with memberships that they were never a party to, and so many other things.

This created a bad impression for the Internet for a while. Detractors shouted from the rooftops about how the Internet was bad and how it should be nipped in the bud.

But the online world was, fortunately, very quick to take reaction. Protective measures were immediately put into place, and quite strong ones at that. Antivirus programs were perfected and a method was devised to keep them regularly updated so that users would be protected from whichever new threats came their way all the time. Not just that, people were protected from online crime with the invention of methods such as antispyware and antimalware applications. More than that, encryption methods were put into place that made people's Internet usage highly secure. Most people found that using the Internet was not like before. They were now working in a highly secure system and their identities were not in jeopardy if they behaved in the right manner!

This is what created a new wave of revolution in Internet usage. Now that this system was highly safe to use, a lot more people began joining in. There was still possibility of Internet crime, but people now knew what they could do to stay safe.

Discovering the World of Web 2.0

By the 2000s, the real evolution of the Internet began. Now almost everyone was on the Internet, and the concept of Web 2.0 slowly began to take shape.

In this new world of Web 2.0, people understood that the best way for them to advance was by sharing information. People understood that they should not keep what they know to themselves, but that they should let others know what they know and the Internet was a wonderful platform for them to do just that. They realized that by giving out information, they got information as well. So, the world of Web 2.0 brought the next new revolution in the Internet world. It showed people that they could give and receive. That they could speak about things they knew and find out about things that they wanted to know.

Web 2.0 is the world of interactivity. The Internet is not passive any more. You do not use it passively. You do not use it for mere input. No one uses it just for that. Now, with the new weapons on the Internet that you have, you can interact with people, with websites and with whole communities if you wanted. You don't need to just sit on your computer chair and see what is there... you can talk to people and you can get connected with them in a way that you cannot do in the real world out there.

Everything that you do on the Internet today is a part of the Web 2.0 thing. You are writing reviews when you like something. You comment on blog posts. If you like a picture that your friend has put up on their profile, you can comment on that. You can vote on things that you like. You can ask for reviews of products that you want to buy. If you read something on a website and want to ask for further information, you can do so on the Internet. You can ask for customer support through the Internet. You can watch videos and then you can vent your feelings about it by commenting on it.

There are just so many different ways in which you can interact on the Internet. But there is more than that. If you like something on the Internet, you have the possibility to subscribe through it via RSS feeds so that you know whenever that particular content is updated. So, you are always kept in the loop. You don't have to worry about forgetting the URL of a great website that you visited. You don't even need to bookmark. You just subscribe to the contents feeds and yo0u are sent messages in your inbox whenever something is updated and then you can go there and visit directly. That's how simplified it has become.

It is true that the Internet and the people on the Internet have become aware of the fact that this whole revolution can be kept going only if people interact with each other. Everybody should get a chance to change things, modify things, ask about things, etc. Even the greatest encyclopedia in the world, Wikipedia, is an open source encyclopedia. Anybody and everybody can edit it. Of course, they have their monitoring and filtering systems because the encyclopedia is something people base their facts on, but the thing to note is that this is something you can change if you want to.

Almost everything that the Internet is today is a part of this Web 2.0 phenomenon. Here we shall take a look at some of those forms.

1. Blogs are the greatest manifestations of this new world of information sharing. The very concept of blogs is that you can put in information and receive it as well. When you make a post on a blog, you are giving out information. You are allowed to share links on blogs as well, which becomes a source for more information. Right now, blogs can be used to upload videos and audio clips, which again means you get more information. Also, blogs are a great resource for distributing eBooks. Many bloggers distribute free eBooks and other resources that can be taken up by people from across the world.

People love blogs because they are regularly updated. Running a blog, as well as reading it, can become a passion. We always love to know what other people think about things, and blogs tell us exactly that. They also allow us to put in our own comments. You can link blogs to several other resources that the Internet has to provide. You can subscribe to the RSS feeds of a blog that you like so that you regularly get to know of any new information that is posted on the blog. You can also add a blog to your social networking profiles. This is a way of recommending a blog to your friends. This works well because people know what you like, and since they know you, it becomes a credible form of marketing for the blogger as well.

2. Another very important way of information sharing in the Web 2.0 world is through viral marketing. Viral marketing is when you like something and then you tell your friends about what you like, so that they can consume it as well.

Suppose you really like a video that you checked out on the Internet. You will naturally want to spread it over on the Internet. You will want to tell your social networking friends about it; if you have a website, you will perhaps want to popularize the video there; you may also want to make your video popular through your blog. We are always like that. If we like something, we want to tell our friends and family about it. We want them to enjoy what we enjoy as well. This is the whole concept of viral marketing. And it works amazingly well. As we shall see very soon, the phenomenon of Web 2.0 has ushered in the world of knowledge marketing. And in that world, the concept of viral marketing works exceedingly well. When you tell people you know about something you like, they are sure to try and check it out.

At least two recent super successes come to my mind when I think about such viral marketing, and both of them are in the field of music. One of them is the American sensation Antoine Dodson. Antoine was interviewed about a family disaster and the way he spoke directly into the camera with unfeigned emotion really bowled over the American audience. Then he came out with a music video which was titled the Bed Intruder Song, featuring himself. This video was put up on YouTube, and it became an instant rage. The video turned him into a celebrity. Why did that happen? The reason was that people who liked his song immediately forwarded the link to their friends, who did the same again. This is a humongous opportunity if you have the right talent, as this boy found out. Never mind if the lyrics are full of profanities and his own inner angst, the point I am trying to make is that people do not flinch from sharing something that they like, and the first people that come to their minds to share something good are the people they know on the Internet.

The other person who attained such superstardom is the British high-pitched soprano, Susan Boyle. This 47 year old, somewhat shy woman appeared on Britain's Got Talent. And while she was fumbling for words during her first audition on the show, with Simon Cowell as one of the judges, everyone felt she would amount to nothing. But this woman had to just open her mouth, and the dream she dreamed went on to become history! The audience gave her a standing ovation, and the people who watched her, immediately put up her video on the Internet. Within just a day, that video got about a million hits, and Susan Boyle became the new generation music diva.

That's the power of the Internet. It is the power of the masses. Now, surely, you will have told your friends about things you like. You will have forwarded links and emails thinking that they should know about it. Whenever you do that, you are using the world of Web 2.0 to the fullest.

Now, these are just two ways in which you are making use of the resources of the Web 2.0 world, probably without even realizing that you are doing so. But, it is happening, and it is an unavoidable trend. You cannot do anything about it. There are so many other ways. When you are checking out a video, writing some comment on your social networking profile, asking for a review on something, checking out a product description on an online store, you are using what Web 2.0 has to offer.

And that brings us to the concept of knowledge marketing. This is something that is all around us, and the people with the most enterprising minds are heavily responsible for making this concept such a big hit in today's world.

These people have realized that the one important reason why such a lot of people are using the Internet is because they are looking for information. This pertains to all kinds of information. There are just so many things out there that everyone is freely dipping into the pool and taking whatever they want from it. Not that anyone is complaining; this is the way the Internet was ordained to be. But you cannot deny that that creates a world of opportunity for everyone. Marketers know that if they give out some information about something, they have a much better ability to sell a product or a service.

Consider someone who has a business relating to a weight loss product. You are going to find tons of such websites out there, because weight loss is one of the commonest things that anyone can find on the Internet. These people know that the most effective way in which they can notch up customers for their business is by giving out information. Check out any of these websites. You will find a barrage of articles about weight loss on each of them.

In fact, do this. Go on Google and look for the keyword „weight loss articles". You are going to find millions of articles out there. Now, open these articles. You will find some good ones, some not-so-good ones and some that are rank bad. But, one thing will be common about them. You will see that all these articles have a little link under them, or somewhere on the page, where they take you for further information. Go there and see what you can find. You will see that when you visit those places for further information, they are whole websites where the main product of the company is being sold!

This is the way marketing works in today's online world. This is the best form of advertising. On the face of it, you are giving out information, and you are actually doing it in the right spirit because most of these articles are definitely very good, but then you are also hooking people to buy your product or business.

The same applies to many of the videos that you will find on YouTube or even any eBook that you download off the Internet. You will find great information in them. They will serve your purpose of finding knowledge and you will certainly have no complaints about them on that count. But then, they will also sell some product or service.

Is anyone complaining about this? Are you feeling bad that you are being sold something in the guise of information? If you are, you shouldn't! No one is complaining about this kind of knowledge marketing. After all, there is no reason to! People who are giving out this content are doing so for free, never mind that they are trying to sell something at the end of it. At least, they do not expect to be paid for what they are telling you. The user is the one benefiting, even if they do not buy the product.

Then there is also the fact that the person who is creating the content is a subject expert. That is because it will only be a subject expert who runs a particular business. They know the ins and outs of the game. So, for the most part, the information that they are giving their readers is good information, information that really makes sense.

That is why you need to consider this aspect closely. There is nothing to crib about. After all, this form of advertising is certainly more meaningful and benevolent than those blatant television commercials that sell products, without giving their users anything of value.

Pardon me for making the Internet marketers seem like a lot of angels who are giving out free information. The truth is that they are also looking for business prospects. At the end of the day, they care about their profits as well. But, the way the Internet has turned out to be right now, it has become a portal of information. So, even if you want to sell something on the Internet, you are not going to go very far if you just want to sell. What you should do is that you should give out information as well—write an article, blog about it, make a video, anything—so that people see the value in it.

Knowledge marketing also helps to build up trust. People begin to trust the person who is giving out all the free content. They establish some kind of relationship with them. They know that they can get what they want from this person.

Also, if they subscribe to their RSS feeds or opt in to their websites or even just bookmark their websites, they can continuously get such free information from them. Eventually, they might decide to become customers for the product, or they might not. But the truth of the matter is that in knowledge marketing, it is the advertised that benefit more than the advertisers.

CHAPTER 7- HOW TO MAKE MONEY ON YOUTUBE

There are lots of ways you are able to make some money on YouTube; however, the method that we will be sharing with you in this chapter is among the easiest. You should know that, recently, YouTube is becoming more of a website where people find information, in addition to being entertained. This gives an ideal chance for Entrepreneurs like us to make money from this huge video site's success. Follow these easy steps and you will easily start making some serious cash very quickly:

Look for a Hot Niche - Popular niches include 'weight loss', 'make money', 'dog training' and 'relationships' to name several. The wonderful thing about YouTube is the large quantity of videos available related to practically any niche.

Next, do some simple searching on the site for videos which are related to your selected niche. Ensure that your niche has a respectable amount of videos (at the very least 50) and that all the videos have view counts in the thousands.

Look for a Product to advertise - This is actually simple to do because you will find large numbers of products available that you can promote being an affiliate. Visit places like Clickbank (as already discussed) and Commission Junction to locate a product related to your niche.

Contact The Owners Of The Most Popular Videos Of Your Niche - Return to all videos you have found which are attracting a consistent stream of viewers and email the owners of those videos. Avoid videos which are promoting things with a website in the video or description.

All you need to do is send the owner a brief email explaining to them that you've got a business proposal that could make them some supplemental income. Explain to them that they should email you back if they're interested.

When they respond, you'll then send another email offering your affiliate link to be placed on their videos. Offer them $20-$30 per month to keep your affiliate URL to the merchandise that you're promoting. You could set-up any type of arrangement - just ensure that it is fair. Your affiliate link will, in all probability, look long and unappealing. You can get your affiliate URL shortened through certain websites.

If the video owner accepts, you're all set. All you must do is send them your link and, when you see that they have placed your link in their video (utilizing annotations in the description), you go and pay him or her in the manner decided. Do not just do that once.

You'll find countless video owners on YouTube who can really make you some nice money.

CHAPTER 8- MAKING MONEY ON THE INTERNET USING YOUR SKILLS AND PASSION

Here is a four-step process that anyone can follow to become successful online:

What Is Your Skill?

The easiest way to make money online is to 'sell' a skill. This skill could be any form of service that you can provide to help other marketers save time, save money and save effort.

Here are a few examples:

Writing – you can become a ghostwriter, copywriter or blogger and sell your skills to other marketers

Graphics Design – you can create powerful E-covers for E-books or graphic banners for mini-sites

Technical – you can help people if you are good with programming (e.g. script installation, testing and website setup)

Networking – help other people to recruit affiliates for their product launches

If you want to develop the winning mindset, make sure you work hard by serving others first even if the pay is low or you are required to sacrifice time (and sometimes, money) in order to develop your skill and build your clientele.

Create Your Own Product

After you develop enough expertise with your skills, you can turn your skills into a product.

The most important thing to remember is that your skill must be something that brings value to others. If you can bring value to others and monetize it, others will most probably want to learn from you as well.

Once you teach others how to monetize their skill, you will have a product that will impart your expertise to others. For example: a product that teaches people "how to make money with copywriting"

Create a Business

Once you are able to combine all your products together and develop your very own system, you have a business running already.

The important thing to remember about a business is that you must have a holistic approach when it comes to business building.

Don't just focus on your primary skill alone. Try and outsource other tasks to other people. For example, if your strength is in writing, your business must not only include writing but many other aspects such as graphics, tutorials and even a helpdesk to help you answer questions.

At the end of the day, you need a complete system to market your business.

Automate Your Business

If your business is taking up too much of your time, the best thing you can do is to try and automate your business by letting others run it for you.

Basically you still maintain ownership of your business (and revenue, of course). But what you must do is to train up people who are capable of running the business for you. By the time your business is successful enough to be automated, you can hire people who are smarter than you to run it for you.

The tradeoff is that you have to pay them a lot of money, but the best thing you have is more free time. When you buy people's time with your money, you effectively remove the shackles that your business has on your time and you can use that time to invest into another business.

Remember the golden rule: Think BIG and think long term.

CHAPTER 9- PITFALLS TO LOOK OUT FOR AS AN INTERNET ENTREPRENEUR

Not Being Proactive

If you truly want to develop a 'think and grow rich' mindset, you must remember that every successful entrepreneur is an ACTION TAKER.

Many make the mistake of building a beautiful website and a product, but they just sit around all day hoping sales will come. This is WRONG.

You must never sit around and wait for things to happen. Rather, you must go out there are recruit partners, make friends and most important of all – DRIVE TRAFFIC!

Forgetting Humanity in the Course of Getting Rich

Another common mistake by Internet marketing newbies – is that they do not spot the hottest trends.

You see, some people are sadly mistaken because they assume that Internet marketing is all about dealing with 'machines'.

At the core of it, the very people who are going to be your customers (or the people who are going to click on your advertisements) are HUMAN BEINGS. We have to apply the proper psychology when we are dealing with them.

Dealing with humans requires the human touch. Are you just writing articles for PEOPLE to read or are you just writing articles to please the search engines?

Thinking of Too Many Things at Once

There are Internet marketers out there who try every traffic generation method in the book but they are not focusing on one.

They try driving in traffic from blogs, search engines, AdWords, viral marketing and everything under the sun, but they are not focused.

It is better to have ONE traffic generation method driving LOTS of traffic compared to 10 traffic generation methods that produce less than one focused method because dabbling with many methods often do not produce concentrated results.

ABOUT THE AUTHOR

Mark is a successful business entrepreneur. He started out with a physical store selling tires and vehicle accessories but soon extended his business online. Today, he enjoys his life in the Caribbean while still making money online.

Mark is definitely living the good life with his wife Maria at this side.

www.ingramcontent.com/pod-product-compliance
Lightning Source LLC
Chambersburg PA
CBHW051237170526
45165CB00004B/1468